ELEPHANTS DON'T LIKE ANTS!

AND OTHER AMAZING FACTS

By Thea Feldman
Illustrated by Lee Cosgrove

Ready-to-Read

SIMON SPOTLIGHT
New York London Toronto Sydney New Delhi
An imprint of Simon & Schuster Children's Publishing Division
1230 Avenue of the Americas, New York, New York 10020
This Simon Spotlight edition August 2021

For information about special discounts for bulk purchases, please contact Simon & Schuster Special Sales at 1-866-506-1949
or business@simonandschuster.com.
Manufactured in the United States of America 0721 LAK
2 4 6 8 10 9 7 5 3
CIP data for this book is available from the Library of Congress.
ISBN 978-1-5344-9633-0 (hc)
ISBN 978-1-5344-9632-3 (pbk)
ISBN 978-1-5344-9634-7 (ebook)

GLOSSARY

habitat: a place where an animal lives in nature

herd: a group of social wild animals, such as elephants

ivory: the material that makes up an elephant's tusks

mammal: an animal that nurses its young with milk

matriarch: the female head of a herd of animals

savanna: a land area where most of the plants are grasses

species: a kind of animal or plant

subspecies: a separate group within a species

tusk: a long, very large tooth that sticks out of an animal's mouth when the mouth is closed

Note to readers: Some of these words may have more than one definition. The definitions above match how these words are used in this book.

CONTENTS

INTRODUCTION 4

CHAPTER 1: 6
AMAZING ELEPHANTS

CHAPTER 2: 10
TRUNK TO TAIL

CHAPTER 3: 22
FOOD, FRIENDS, AND FAMILY

ELEPHANTS IN TROUBLE 32

INTRODUCTION

Did you know that elephants are the world's largest land animal?

Asian elephant

They also have amazing memories and use their tusks like tools.

This may sound funny, but even though elephants are HUGE, they are also scared of ants.

African forest elephant

Elephants are amazing in many other ways too. By the time you finish this book, you will know an ENORMOUS amount about what makes elephants so super!

CHAPTER 1

AMAZING ELEPHANTS

The places where animals live in nature are called habitats. In the wild, elephants make their homes on grasslands and in forests, savannas, swamps, deserts, and highlands.

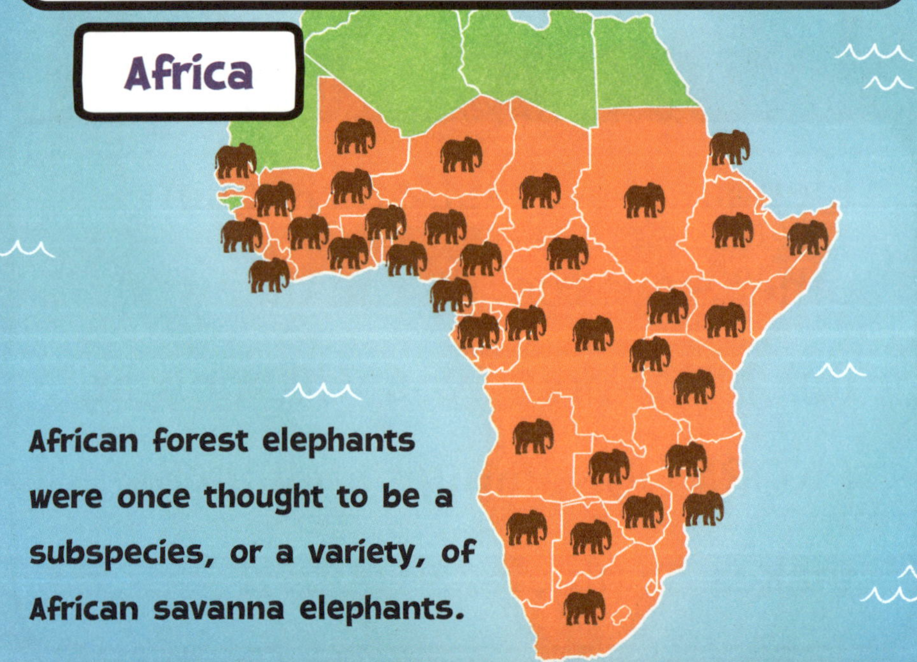

African forest elephants were once thought to be a subspecies, or a variety, of African savanna elephants.

Asian elephants live in forested areas and grasslands.

African savanna elephants live on grasslands called savannas.

African forest elephants live in forested areas.

Elephants are the largest land animals. Even so, African elephants have a HUGE problem with one of the world's tiniest animals—ants.

Male African savanna elephants weigh up to 14,000 pounds.

Male African forest elephants weigh between 5,000 and 10,000 pounds.

Elephants love to munch on acacia trees, but the ants that live in the trees bite and sting to keep elephants away!

Ouch! The only place I want an ant is at the end of my name!

Male Asian elephants weigh around 11,000 pounds.

CHAPTER 2

TRUNK TO TAIL

Do you want to know an easy way to tell an African elephant from an Asian elephant?

Check out their ears!

An African elephant's ears are much bigger, and are shaped like Africa!

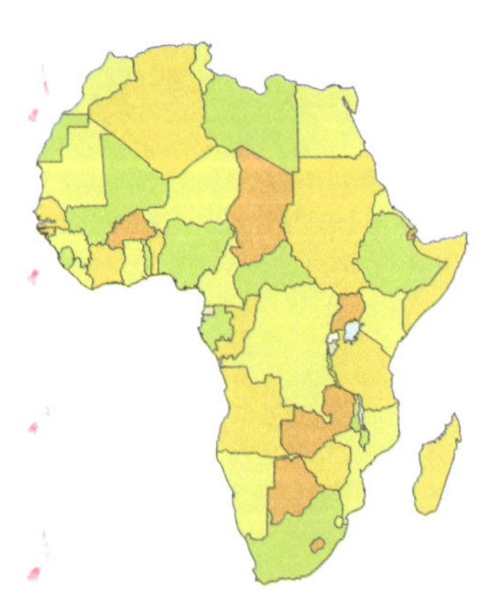

An African elephant's ear can be six feet long from top to bottom and can weigh a hundred pounds.

The elephant's ears make excellent fans in the African heat. If you see an elephant flapping its ears, it's cooling off!

An elephant packs a whole lot of uses into its trunk! An elephant trunk works as both an upper lip and a nose.

A trunk is like a straw that can hold up to 2.5 gallons of water.
Elephants even greet each other with their trunks!
An elephant's trunk is strong enough to push down trees but delicate enough to pick up food or a single piece of straw!

An elephant's trunk has no bones, sixteen major muscles, and about 40,000 smaller muscles. A male African elephant's trunk can be almost seven feet long.

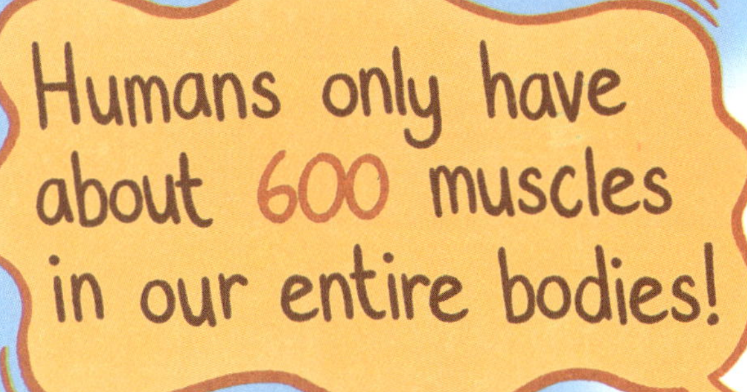

There is one tip at the end of an Asian elephant's trunk. The African elephant has two.

African elephant

Asian elephant

An elephant's tusks work like tools. Elephants use them to lift and carry things, to defend themselves, to dig water holes, and to strip bark from trees.

The longest tusk on record was 11.5 feet!

A forest elephant's tusks tend to point straight down.

Adult female Asian elephants do not have tusks.

One tusk often gets more worn down than the other, because elephants use one tusk more than the other!

Tusks are actually two upper teeth. Unlike human teeth, elephant tusks never stop growing unless they break in such a way that the root is damaged.

Look at the rounded shape of an African elephant's head. An Asian elephant's head has two domes on top. This is another way you can tell the two species apart.

An elephant's eyeballs are only about one and a half inches wide. That's just a bit larger than a human eye!

An elephant's eyelashes, however, can be up to five inches long! They help to keep dust and sand out of its eyes.

Elephants are born blind. A baby elephant often holds on to its mother's tail as it walks, until its sight develops.

An elephant's brain weighs between eight and thirteen pounds, which makes it the largest brain of any land mammal.

The part of the elephant's brain that is important for high brain function is also the largest of any land mammal.

Among other things, this means an elephant has a really good memory. It will remember food and water sources and other things key to surviving in the wild.

Elephants remember each other even if they've been apart for decades.

CHAPTER 3

FOOD, FRIENDS, AND FAMILY

Elephants sometimes spend between twelve and eighteen hours a day eating. They consume about three hundred pounds of food every day.

A Vegetarian Diet

Elephant teeth wear down from all those hours of grinding food, and then new teeth replace them. An elephant tooth can be a foot long and weigh up to eight pounds!

Elephants live together in groups called herds. The oldest female leads the herd and is called the matriarch (say: MAY-tree-ark).

The matriarch leads the herd to food and water every day.

Each herd is made up of adult females and young elephants. All the adult elephants work together to help raise the young.

Adult herd members keep young elephants safe from danger.
An elephant is pregnant for 22 months.
A newborn baby elephant weighs about 200 pounds.

Female elephants stay with the herd their whole lives.

Male elephants leave the herd they were born into when they are between twelve and fifteen years old. They may join a smaller herd of other males of the same age until it is time to mate.

Elephants are also extremely intelligent.

They use mud as sunscreen and twigs as flyswatters, and are one of the few species to recognize themselves in a mirror!

Elephants can live for around 70 years. When an elephant dies, the other elephants in its herd mourn its death. This is another example of how complex and special elephants are.

If you could be an elephant, what would you do with your trunk and your tusks?

Would you be excited to have an amazing memory? Would you run away from ants?

Elephants are awesome, but what do you think is the most amazing thing about them? It's up to you!

Turn the page to learn how to protect elephants!

Elephants are peaceful giants that don't threaten other animals or people. Unfortunately, elephants are in danger in the wild from both the loss of their habitat and the international trade in ivory, which is the material that makes up an elephant's tusks.

Ivory has long been used to make things such as jewelry, pool balls, piano keys, and more. Laws have been passed to make it illegal for people to kill elephants for their ivory tusks, but each year thousands of elephants are still killed by people trying to make money off the crime. Governments around the world, including the United States and China, have passed strict laws banning sales of ivory. Governments in countries where elephants live are trying to provide alternative job opportunities to working in the ivory trade.

If you want to help protect elephants, make sure you and your family don't buy any products made of ivory. Consider holding a bake sale or other fundraiser for an organization that helps elephants.